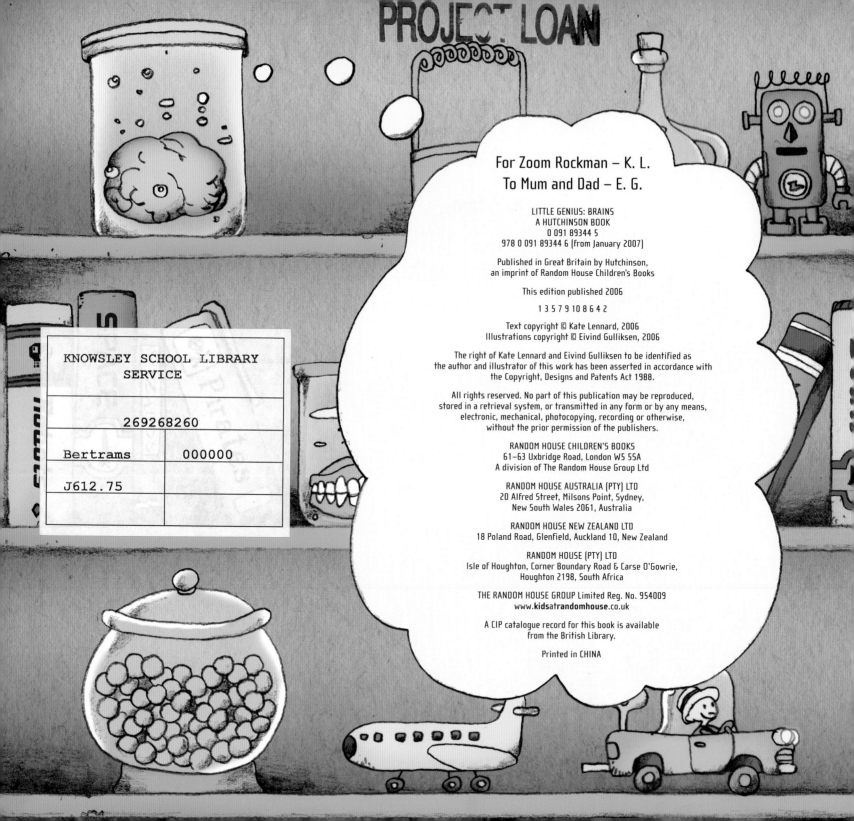

For Zoom Rockman – K. L.
To Mum and Dad – E. G.

LITTLE GENIUS: BRAINS
A HUTCHINSON BOOK
0 091 89344 5
978 0 091 89344 6 (from January 2007)

Published in Great Britain by Hutchinson,
an imprint of Random House Children's Books

This edition published 2006

1 3 5 7 9 10 8 6 4 2

RANDOM HOUSE CHILDREN'S BOOKS
61–63 Uxbridge Road, London W5 5SA
A division of The Random House Group Ltd

RANDOM HOUSE AUSTRALIA (PTY) LTD
20 Alfred Street, Milsons Point, Sydney,
New South Wales 2061, Australia

RANDOM HOUSE NEW ZEALAND LTD
18 Poland Road, Glenfield, Auckland 10, New Zealand

RANDOM HOUSE (PTY) LTD
Isle of Houghton, Corner Boundary Road & Carse O'Gowrie,
Houghton 2198, South Africa

THE RANDOM HOUSE GROUP Limited Reg. No. 954009
www.kidsatrandomhouse.co.uk

A CIP catalogue record for this book is available
from the British Library.

Printed in CHINA

PROJECT LOAN

Hello!
I'm **Little Genius**.

I've been looking into the human body, and all the interesting bits that make it work.

This book is about the amazing machine inside your head called your

brain.

I'm here to tell you all about it . . .

Inside your head,
behind your eyes,
is an amazing machine
called your **brain.**

Your brain
has a wiggly,
wrinkled surface.

If you were to iron out all the wrinkles,
there would be enough material to make this
alien outfit . . .

CooL!

If you could touch your brain,
it would feel wet and wobbly,
like a **big pink jelly**.

Jelly can squash really easily . . .

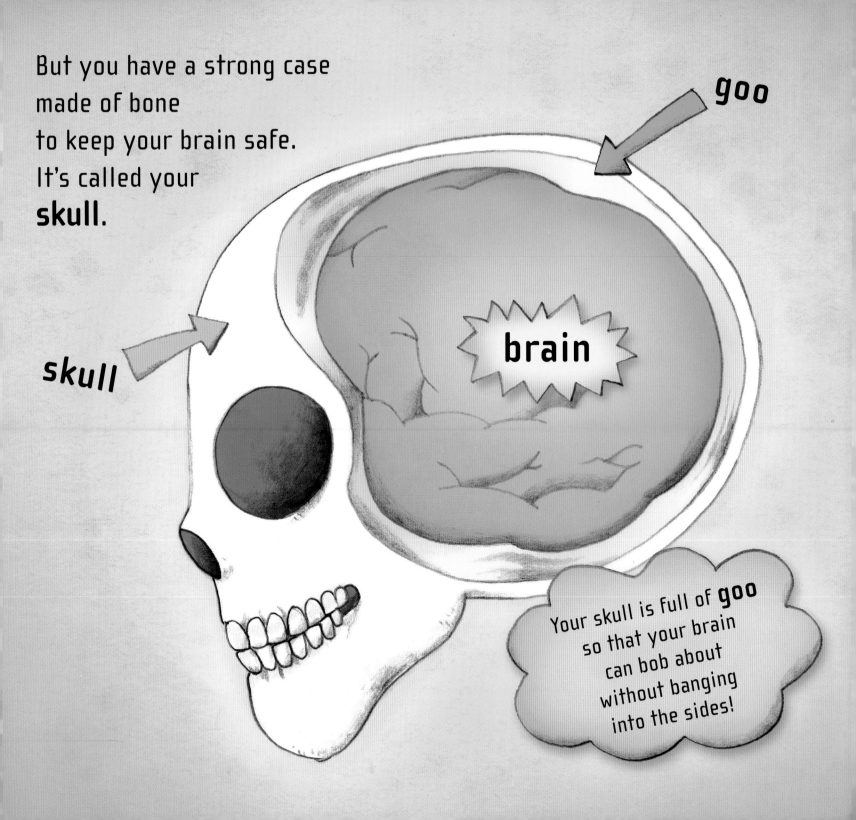

But you have a strong case
made of bone
to keep your brain safe.
It's called your
skull.

goo

skull

brain

Your skull is full of **goo** so that your brain can bob about without banging into the sides!

Imagine that your head is this boiled egg.

If you were to take off the top, you would see your brain. It would look like this.

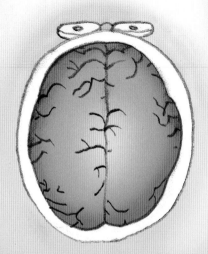

Your brain is made up of two halves.

The left half works everything on the right side of your body.

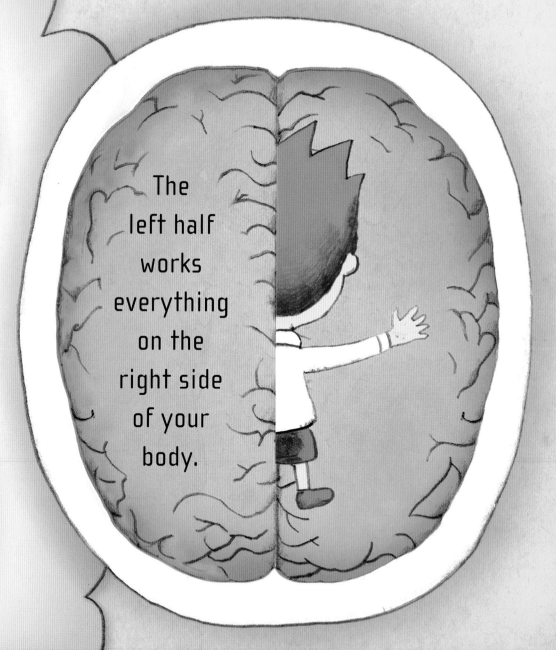

It is possible to look at your brain without taking it out of your head.

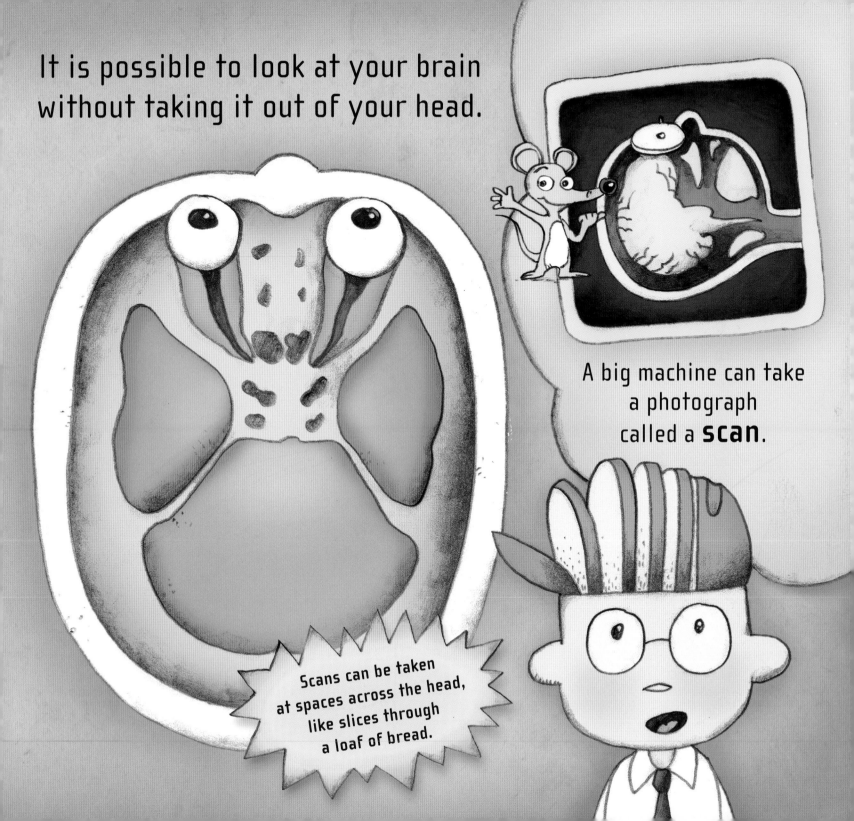

A big machine can take a photograph called a **scan**.

Scans can be taken at spaces across the head, like slices through a loaf of bread.

Here is another view of the brain,
this time from the side.

The long bit at the bottom is called the **brainstem.**

It's a bit like
the stem
of a flower.

The brainstem
pokes down
through your neck.
Its job is to carry
the right amount
of blood and air
up to your brain.

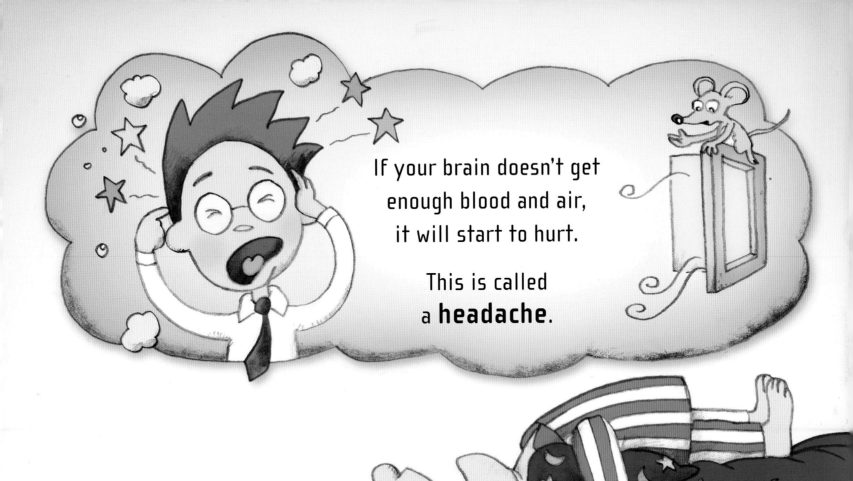

If your brain doesn't get enough blood and air, it will start to hurt.

This is called a **headache**.

You can get a headache if you sleep with your neck in a funny position like this.

Every creature has a brain:

fish

elephants

monkeys

giraffes

squirrels

even this tiny flea!

Animals with bigger brains aren't always more clever than those with smaller ones.

This clever bee knows how to make delicious honey.

But this silly cow is standing in her own poo **again!**

Humans are very clever.
But other animals are clever too,
like these smart little
dolphins.

They can understand
sign language
and do fantastic tricks.

And they can answer
simple questions like,
Do you want a fish?

or,
*Do you want a bucket
on your head?*

Dolphins speak to each other by making funny whistling and clicking noises. Unfortunately, nobody knows what they're talking about. So it's hard to find out *just* how clever they are.

We do know that a dolphin can find its way around underwater – even in the darkest places at the bottom of the ocean – like a **submarine**. Now that is **clever!**

A baby's brain is as heavy as an **apple**.

My brain is as heavy as a **potato**.

A teacher's brain is as heavy as a **pumpkin**.

And a bird's brain is as heavy as half a **pea**!

You use your brain
when you need
to remember something,
like your address
or what you had for breakfast.

Your brain stores
the memory
deep inside.
This is called
learning.

If you are trying to learn something **new**, like the name of this **planet**, try **saying** it **over** and **over** again, closing your **eyes** and **seeing** it as a *picture*.

SATURN

BuzzZZZZZz

SATURN is yellow
with amazing stripy rings,
so think of yourself
'sat on' a bumble bee.

That should help
the memory to stick!

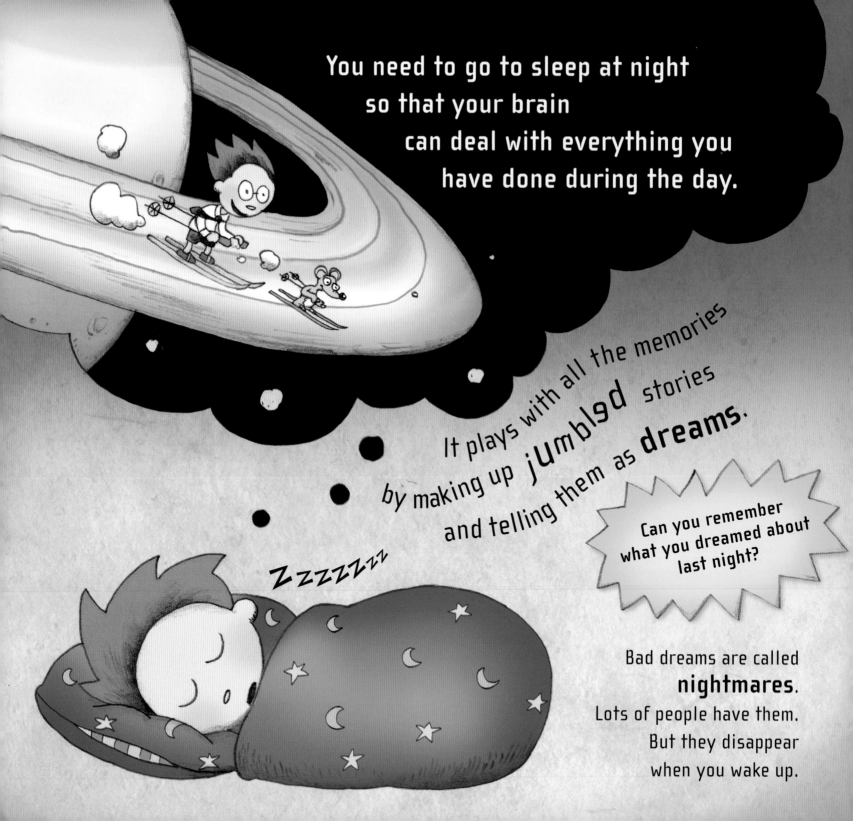

You need to go to sleep at night
so that your brain
can deal with everything you
have done during the day.

It plays with all the memories
by making up jumbled stories
and telling them as **dreams**.

Zzzzzzz

Can you remember
what you dreamed about
last night?

Bad dreams are called
nightmares.
Lots of people have them.
But they disappear
when you wake up.

The more you learn,
the quicker your brain will be
at remembering things,
and coming up with answers
to puzzles like these . . .

How many more words
can you make out of the letters,
B R A I N?

rain   ban   an   nib

Which brain
is the same as this one?

Which brain
belongs to which body?

Sometimes you can picture things in your head that nobody has ever seen before.
This is called **imagination**.

Looking

Some people are rubbish at puzzles but have brilliant imaginations.

They can think up ideas and tell them as drawings and paintings,
or write them as stories.

YUM!

Tasting

Reading is very good for your imagination.
New words and ideas help your brain grow strong and clever.

Listening

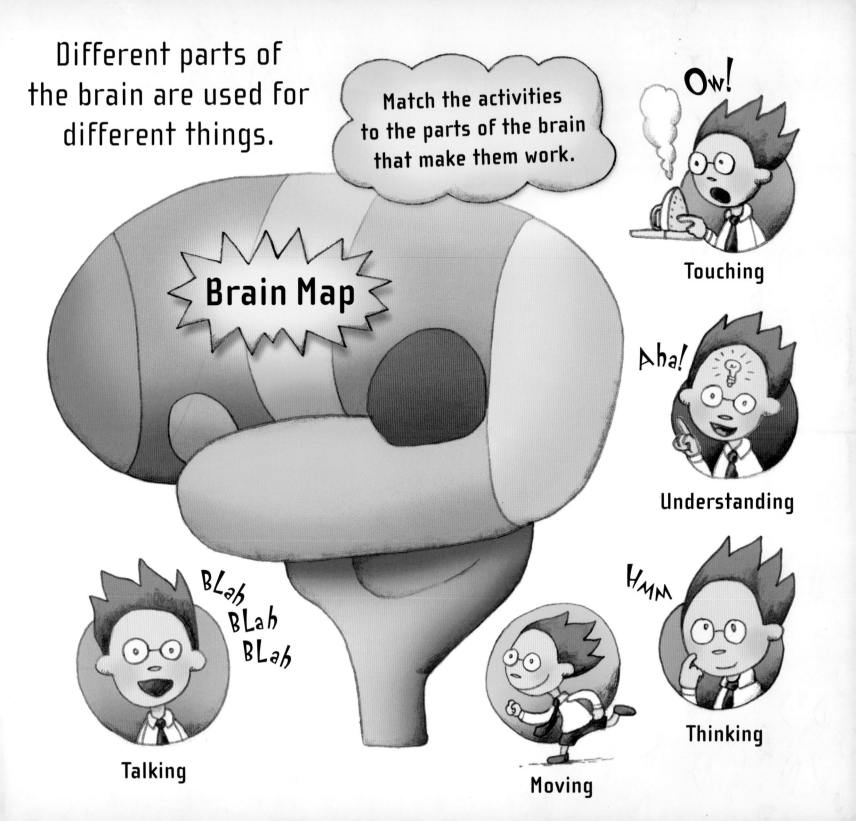

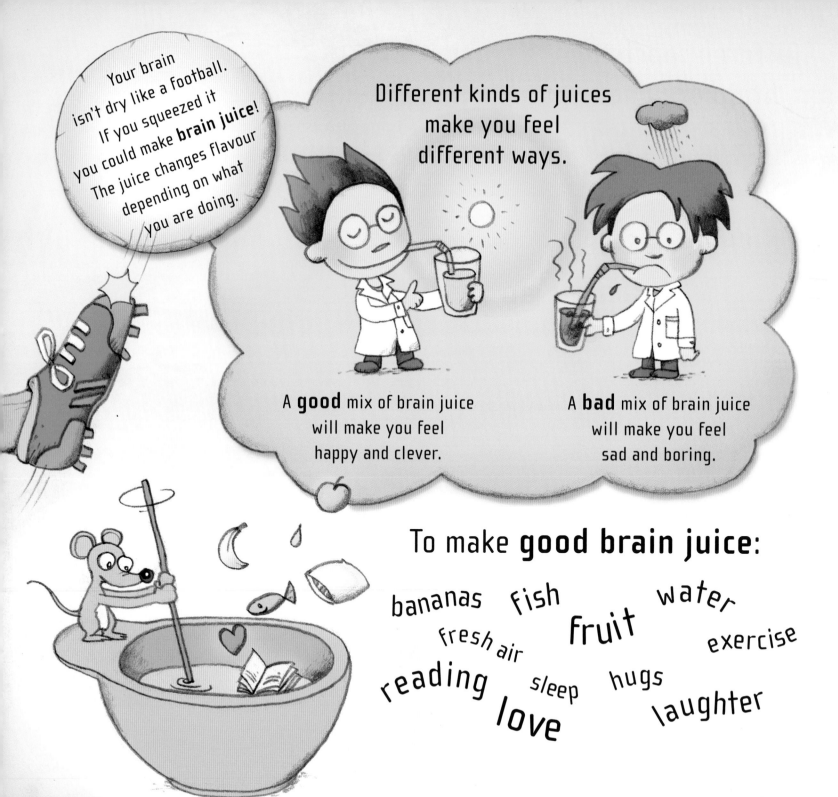

A damaged brain can't mend itself like a cut finger.

Some people wear special hats to protect their brains when they are working.

policemen

builders

Firemen

And when they are having fun.

skaters

cyclists

If you ride a bike, don't forget to wear a **helmet**.

You don't want to end up with a brain like **scrambled egg!**

I'm going to really look after my brain.

I don't just use it to say clever things.
I use it to think of funny riddles too, like,

How do two brains say goodbye?

With a **BRAIN WAVE!**

Goodbye!

That was everything I found out about **brains**.

This man knows a lot about brains.
He's a **brain surgeon**.

A brain surgeon
is a special type of doctor
who mends people's brains
if they aren't working properly.

To be a brain surgeon
you need to have
lots of good
brain juice.

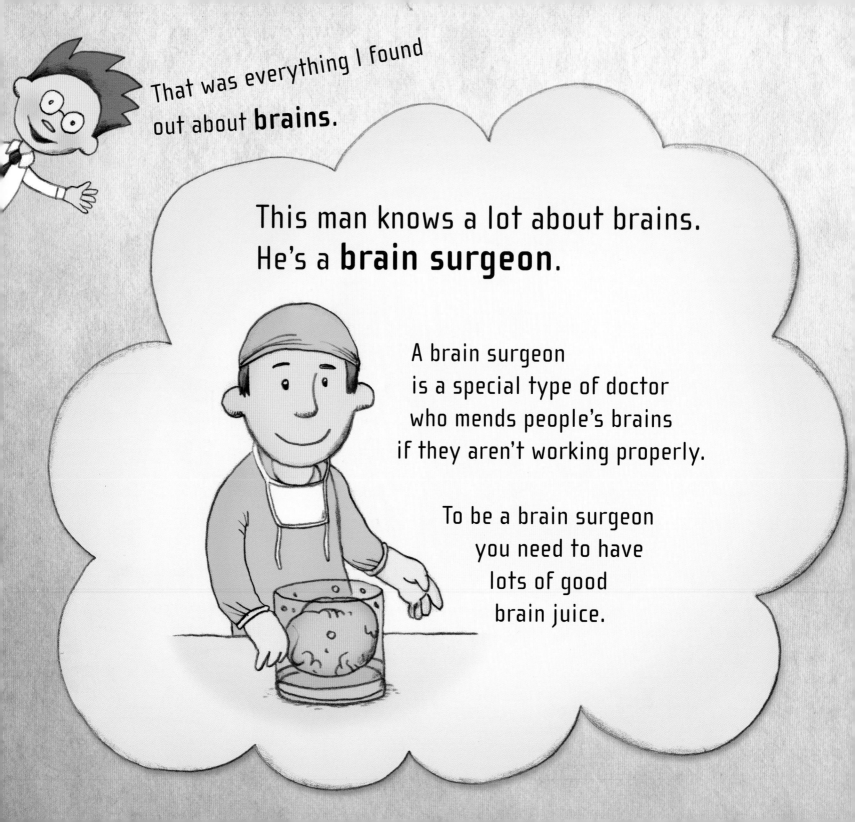

I'd like to be
a brain surgeon
when I grow up.

Would you?